Name

Address

Blank Classic

Dotted Bullet Journal
113 numbered pages - 120 total pages
A5 (5.83 x 8.27)

Design © 2020 Blank Classics

Blank Classic

Mailing address:
Blank Classic
PO BOX 4608
Main Station Terminal
349 West Georgia Street
Vancouver, BC
Canada, V6B 4A1

Cover design by: Lauren Dick

ISBN: 978-1-77437-969-1

FIRST EDITION / FIRST PRINTING

— Contents —

Page	Topic

— Contents —

Page	Topic
Page	Topic

— Contents —

Page	Topic

— Contents —

Page	Topic
Page	